LOVE SEX AND LASTING RELATIONSHIPS

GOD'S PRESCRIPTION FOR ENHANCING YOUR LOVE LIFE

CHIP INGRAM

LOVE, SEX AND LASTING RELATIONSHIPS

Table of Contents

How to Start Your Own Small Group

The fact that you are even reading this page says a lot about you. It says that you are either one of those people that has to read everything, or it says you are open to God using you to lead a group.

Leading a small group can sound intimidating, but it really doesn't have to be. Think of it more as gathering a few friends to get to know each other better and to have some discussion around biblical truths.

Here are a few practical tips to help you get started:

1. PRAY – One of the most important principles of spiritual leadership is to realize you can't do this on your own. No matter how long you've been a Christian or been involved in ministry, you need the power of the Holy Spirit. Lean on Him… He will help you.

2. INVITE SOME FRIENDS – Don't be afraid to ask people to come to your group. You will be surprised how many people are open to a study like this. Whether you have 4 of 14 in your group, it can be a powerful experience. You should probably plan on at least an hour and a half for your group meeting.

3. GET YOUR MATERIALS – You will need to get a DVD of the video teaching done by Chip Ingram. You can get the DVD from livingontheedge.org. Also, it will be helpful for each person to have their own study guide. You can also purchase those through the Living on the Edge website.

4. BE PREPARED TO FACILITATE – Just a few minutes a week in preparation can make a huge difference in the group experience. Each week preview the video teaching and review the discussion questions. If you don't think your group can get through all the questions, select the ones that are most relevant to your group.

5. LEARN TO SAY "I DON'T KNOW." – When tough questions come up, it's ok for you to say "I don't know." Take the pressure off. No one expects you to have all the answers.

6. LOVE YOUR GROUP – Maybe the most important thing you bring to the group is your personal care for them. If you will pray for them, encourage them, call them, e-mail them, involve them, and love them, God will be pleased and you will have a lot of fun along the way.

Thank you for your availability. May God bless you as you serve Him by serving others.

How to Get the Most Out of This Experience

Every one of us is wired to love and be loved. We were made and designed by our creator to experience relationships that have deep emotional and spiritual connection. And within marriage, God created us to enjoy great sex. During this series you will discover how to do love, sex, and relationships God's way.

Listed below are the segments you will experience each week as well as some hints for getting the most out of this experience. If you are leading the group, you will find some additional help and coaching tips on pages 83–95. Video coaching is also available under the Coaching menu on the DVD as well as at livingontheedge.org. Click "Small Groups and Coaching."

Take It In (Watch the Video)

It is important for us to get "before God" and submit ourselves to His truth. During this section you will watch the video teaching by Chip.

A teaching outline with fill-ins is provided for each session. As you follow along, write down questions or insights that you can share during the discussion time.

Even though most of the verses will appear on the screen and in your notes, it is a great idea to bring your own Bible each week. It will allow you to make notes in your own Bible and find other passages that might be relevant to that week's study.

Talk It Over

We not only grow by listening to God's word, but we grow "in community." The friendship and insights of those in the group will enrich your small group experience. Several discussion questions are provided for your group to further engage the teaching content. Keep the following guidelines in mind for having a healthy group discussion.

- Be involved. Jump in and share your thoughts. Your ideas are important, and you have a perspective that is unique and can benefit the other group members.

- Be a good listener. Value what others are sharing. Seek to really understand the perspective of others in your group and don't be afraid to ask follow up questions.

- Be courteous. Spirited discussion is great. Disrespect and attack is not. When there is disagreement, focus on the issue and never turn the discussion into a personal attack.

- Be focused. Stay on topic. Help the group explore the subject at hand, and try to save unrelated questions or stories for afterwards.

- Be careful not to dominate. Be aware of the amount of talking you are doing in proportion to the rest of the group, and make space for others to speak.

- Be a learner. Stay sensitive to what God might be wanting to teach you through the lesson, as well as through what others have to say. Focus more on your own growth rather than making a point or winning an argument.

LIVE IT OUT – BIO

BIO is a word that is synonymous with "life." Found in those three simple letters B.I.O. is the key to helping you become the person God wants you to be.

B = Come "BEFORE GOD" daily – To meet with Him personally through His Word and prayer, to enjoy His presence, receive His direction, and follow His will.

I = Do Life "IN COMMUNITY" weekly – Structuring your week to personally connect in safe relationships that provide love, support, transparency, challenge, and accountability.

O = Be "ON MISSION" 24/7 – Cultivating a mindset to "live out" Jesus' love for others through acts of sacrifice and service at home, work, play, and church.

ACCELERATE (20 Minutes That Turn Concepts Into Convictions)

Inspiration comes from hearing God's Word; motivation grows by discussing God's Word; transformation occurs when you study it for yourself.

If you want to "accelerate" your growth, a short bible study is provided that you can do at home each week. Our convictions become even stronger when we dig into Scripture and discover truth for ourselves. To help you get the most out of this exercise, consider partnering up with somebody in your group who will also commit to do the assignment this week. Then, after you have each done the assignment, agree to spend 10-15 minutes by phone to share what you learned and what you are applying.

Session 1

THE SECRET TO A LASTING RELATIONSHIP

Part 1

THE SECRET TO A LASTING RELATIONSHIP
Ephesians 5:1-2

Take It In (Watch the Video)

HOLLYWOOD'S PRESCRIPTION FOR LASTING RELATIONSHIPS

A. Four Steps to Follow

1. _____ the right person.

2. _____ in love.

3. _____ your hopes and dreams on this person for your future fulfillment.

4. If _____ occurs, repeat steps 1, 2, and 3.

B. The Success Rate

C. The Pain, the Fallout and the Damage

GOD'S PRESCRIPTION FOR LASTING RELATIONSHIPS

Therefore be imitators of God, as beloved children; and walk in love, just as Christ also loved you and gave Himself up for us, an offering and a sacrifice to God as a fragrant aroma.

Ephesians 5:1-2 (NASB)

Talk It Over

1. "What are the most dominant messages from Hollywood about love, sex, and relationships?"

_____

_____

_____

_____

Judith S. Wallerstein, The Unexpected
Legacy of Divorce

2. How have you seen the cultural messages about love and sex change during your lifetime?

    _____

    _____

    _____

3. Chip said that believing these messages from Hollywood about love and sex destine us to fail in our relationships. Why would that be true?

    _____

    _____

    _____

4. How does having your identity securely rooted in Christ impact your view of love and sex?

    _____

    _____

    _____

Live It Out – B.I.O.

BIO is a word that is synonymous with "life." Found in those three simple letters B.I.O. is the key to helping you become the person God wants you to be.

B = Come BEFORE GOD daily – To meet with Him personally through His word and prayer to enjoy His presence, receive His direction, and follow His will.

I = Do Life IN COMMUNITY weekly – Structuring your week to personally connect in safe relationships that provide love, support, transparency, challenge, and accountability.

O = Be ON MISSION 24/7 – Cultivating a mindset to "live out" Jesus' love for others through acts of sacrifice and service at home, work, play, and church.

COME BEFORE GOD

5. Ephesians 5:1 (NASB) says "Therefore be imitators of God, as beloved children; and walk in love…" What does being an "imitator" of God have to do with our relationships?

_____

_____

_____

DO LIFE IN COMMUNITY

6. Paul says in Ephesians 5 that we are God's "beloved" children. Chip said that we are "deeply loved." What are the biggest barriers to creating a group where people feel deeply loved?

_____

_____

_____

BE ON MISSION

7. Chip defined love as choosing to give another person what they need the most when they deserve it the least at great personal cost. If we really began to live out that definition of love, how would it change our relationships?

_____

_____

_____

Accelerate (20 Minutes That Turn Concepts Into Convictions)

INSPIRATION comes from hearing God' Word; MOTIVATION grows by discussing God's Word; TRANSFORMATION occurs when you study it for yourself.

If you want to "accelerate" your growth, here is an assignment you can do this week. To help you get the most out of this exercise, consider partnering up with somebody in your group who will also commit to do the assignment this week. Then, after you have each done the assignment, agree to spend 10 minutes by phone to share what you learned and what you are applying.

COME BEFORE GOD

1. Carefully and slowly read the following passage from Ephesians 1:3-14 (NIV). On one occasion an expert in the law stood up to test Jesus. "Teacher," he asked, "what must I do to inherit eternal life?"

   Praise be to the God and Father of our Lord Jesus Christ, who has blessed us in the heavenly realms with every spiritual blessing in Christ. For he chose us in him before the creation of the world to be holy and blameless in his sight. In love he predestined us for adoption to sonship through Jesus Christ, in accordance with his pleasure and will— to the praise of his glorious grace, which he has freely given us in the One he loves. In him we have redemption through his blood, the forgiveness of sins, in accordance with the riches of God's grace that he lavished on us. With all wisdom and understanding, he made known to us the mystery of his will according to his good pleasure, which he purposed in Christ, to be put into effect when the times reach their fulfillment—to bring unity to all things in heaven and on earth under Christ.

   In him we were also chosen, having been predestined according to the plan of him who works out everything in conformity with the purpose of his will, in order that we, who were the first to put our hope in Christ, might be for the praise of his glory. And you also were included in Christ when you heard the message of truth, the gospel of your salvation. When you believed, you were marked in him with a seal, the promised Holy Spirit, who is a deposit guaranteeing our inheritance until the redemption of those who are God's possession—to the praise of his glory.

2. Go through this passage and make a list of all the spiritual blessings that are yours in Christ Jesus.

_____

_____

_____

3. Paul says in this passage that we have been "adopted into sonship." When a child is adopted into a family, what changes?

    •

    •

    •

    •

    •

4. Spend some time this week meditating on these spiritual blessings. Let them soak into you spirit and lead you to more deeply embrace how much you are loved.

DO LIFE IN COMMUNITY

6. Send a note or an e-mail to a friend this week and let them know how deeply loved they are by God and by you.

BE ON MISSION

7. How does understanding who you are in Christ impact the way you live the Christian life and the way you treat other people?

_____

_____

_____

Session 2

THE SECRET TO A LASTING RELATIONSHIP

Part 2

THE SECRET TO A LASTING RELATIONSHIP, PT. 2
Ephesians 5:1-2

Take It In (Watch the Video)

GOD'S PRESCRIPTION FOR LASTING RELATIONSHIPS

Therefore be imitators of God, as beloved children; and walk in love, just as Christ also loved you and gave Himself up for us, an offering and a sacrifice to God as a fragrant aroma.

Ephesians 5:1-2 (NASB)

A. Four Steps to Follow

1. _____ the right person.

2. _____ in love.

3. _____ your hope on God and seek to please Him through this relationship.

4. If _____ occurs, repeat steps 1, 2, and 3.

B. The Success Rate

C. The Reward, the Legacy and the Blessing

PICTORIAL SUMMARY
Two Models For Lasting Relationships

God's Prescription

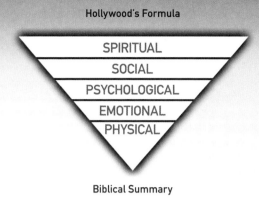

Hollywood's Formula

Biblical Summary

Do not conform to the pattern of this world, but be transformed by the renewing of your mind. Then you will be able to test and approve what God's will is—his good, pleasing and perfect will.

Romans 12:2 (NIV)

Talk It Over

1. In this session Chip said "The greatest thing I do for my wife every single day is to pursue passionately my relationship with Christ." Why is that true? And when I pursue Jesus first, how does that positively impact my marriage or other relationships?

_____

_____

_____

2. Chip said "We need to become what we want." What is one area where you would like to grow in that will help you "become the right person"?

_____

_____

_____

3. What is the difference between Hollywood's view of "falling in love" and Paul's challenge to "walk in love"?

_____

_____

_____

4. Chip said "You can only walk in love when you feel loved." What do you think he means by that statement?

_____

_____

_____

Live It Out – B.I.O.

BIO is a word that is synonymous with "life." Found in those three simple letters B.I.O. is the key to helping you become the person God wants you to be.

B = Come BEFORE GOD daily – To meet with Him personally through His word and prayer to enjoy His presence, receive His direction, and follow His will.

I = Do Life IN COMMUNITY weekly – Structuring your week to personally connect in safe relationships that provide love, support, transparency, challenge, and accountability.

O = Be ON MISSION 24/7 – Cultivating a mindset to "live out" Jesus' love for others through acts of sacrifice and service at home, work, play, and church.

COME BEFORE GOD

5. In Ephesians 4:31-32 (NIV) Paul says, "Get rid of all bitterness, rage and anger, brawling and slander, along with every form of malice. Be kind and compassionate to one another, forgiving each other, just as in Christ God forgave you."

Which of these issues do you most need to work on in your relationships?

_____

_____

_____

DO LIFE IN COMMUNITY

6. Chip read the quote that says "If you attempt to build intimacy with another person before you have done the hard work of becoming a whole and healthy person, every relationship will be an attempt to complete the wholeness that you lack and end in disaster."

   How can this group help you be a more "whole and healthy person"?

   _____

   _____

   _____

BE ON MISSION

7. At the end of the session Chip talked about reward, legacy and blessing. When it comes to love and sex, what kind of legacy do you want to leave for your kids, grandkids, and friends?

   _____

   _____

   _____

Drs. Les & Leslie Parrott, Relatoinships, 20

Accelerate (20 Minutes That Turn Concepts Into Convictions)

INSPIRATION comes from hearing God' Word; MOTIVATION grows
by discussing God's Word; TRANSFORMATION occurs when you study it for
yourself.

If you want to "accelerate" your growth, here is an assignment you can do this
week. To help you get the most out of this exercise, consider partnering up with
somebody in your group who will also commit to do the assignment this week.
Then, after you have each done the assignment, agree to spend 10 minutes by
phone to share what you learned and what you are applying.

COME BEFORE GOD

1. Chip talked this week about the importance of "becoming the right person."
    Carefully and slowly read the following passage in light of that statement.

    So I tell you this, and insist on it in the Lord, that you must no longer live
    as the Gentiles do, in the futility of their thinking. They are darkened in
    their understanding and separated from the life of God because of the
    ignorance that is in them due to the hardening of their hearts. Having
    lost all sensitivity, they have given themselves over to sensuality so as to
    indulge in every kind of impurity, and they are full of greed.

    That, however, is not the way of life you learned when you heard about
    Christ and were taught in him in accordance with the truth that is in
    Jesus. You were taught, with regard to your former way of life, to put
    off your old self, which is being corrupted by its deceitful desires; to
    be made new in the attitude of your minds; and to put on the new
    self, created to be like God in true righteousness and holiness.

    Therefore each of you must put off falsehood and speak truthfully to
    your neighbor, for we are all members of one body. "In your anger do not
    sin": Do not let the sun go down while you are still angry, and do not give
    the devil a foothold. Anyone who has been stealing must steal no longer,
    but must work, doing something useful with their own hands, that they
    may have something to share with those in need.

    Do not let any unwholesome talk come out of your mouths, but only what
    is helpful for building others up according to their needs, that it may
    benefit those who listen. And do not grieve the Holy Spirit of God, with
    whom you were sealed for the day of redemption. Get rid of all bitterness,

rage and anger, brawling and slander, along with every form of malice. Be kind and compassionate to one another, forgiving each other, just as in Christ God forgave you.

Ephesians 4:17-32 (NIV)

2. According to verses 17-19, what are some of the markers (characteristics) of people who don't know Christ?

_____

_____

_____

3. Circle all of the words in verses 20-23 that indicate "becoming the right person" is a "process."

_____

_____

_____

4. What is meant by the phrase "old self"? And, what does it look like practically to "put off" the old self?

_____

_____

_____

DO LIFE IN COMMUNITY

5. Paul said not to let any unwholesome talk come out of our mouths. Get together with a friend this week and let them know where you need to be more accountable when it comes to your "tongue."

BE ON MISSION

6. Commit this week to put into practice the first words of Ephesians 4:32... "be kind and compassionate to one another".

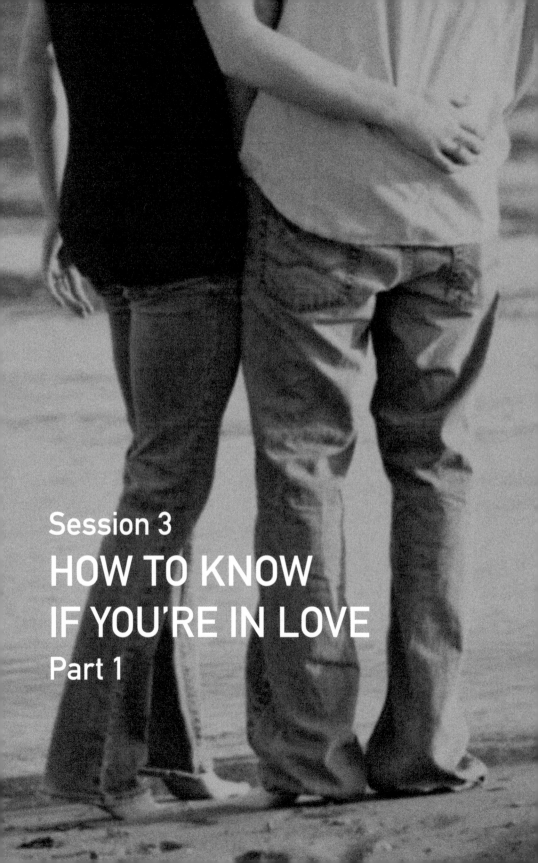

Session 3

HOW TO KNOW
IF YOU'RE IN LOVE

Part 1

HOW TO KNOW IF YOU'RE IN LOVE
Ephesians 5:1-2

Take It In (Watch the Video)

Introduction – Three Kinds of Love

1. EROS LOVE – This is need love. It is based upon physical attraction and fulfillment. This love is necessary for marriage to succeed; however, marriage cannot be sustained by eros alone. – Proverbs 5:15-19

2. PHILEO LOVE – This is friendship love. The Bible uses the word "companionship" several times in describing what a marriage relationship is. Phileo love means reciprocal sharing of time, activities, the home, hobbies, games, and other objects of common fellowship. – Romans 12:9-13

3. AGAPE LOVE – This is a giving love. This can be unilateral in that one loves even when the other doesn't respond as expected. It is self-giving in meeting real needs of the other with the purpose of helping the person to become a better, more mature individual. Agape love takes the initiative and energizes the other two kinds of love. Agape's characteristics are in 1 Corinthians 13:4-8.

Test #1 - TIME

- Love grows, and all growth requires time.

- Infatuation may come suddenly.

Test #2 - KNOWLEDGE

- Love grows out of an appraisal of all the known characteristics of the other person.

- Infatuation may arise from an acquaintance with only a few or only one of these characteristics.

Test #3 – FOCUS

- Love is other-person-centered. It is outgoing. It results in sharing.

- Infatuation is self-centered.

Test #4 – SINGULARITY

- Genuine love is centered on one person only.

Dr. Michael Liebowitz, Chemistry of Love, NY State Psychiatric Institute

- An infatuated individual may be "in love" with two or more persons simultaneously.

Test #5 – SECURITY

- An individual in love tends to have a sense of security and a feeling of trust after considering everything involved in his relationship with the other person.

- An infatuated individual tends to have a blind sense of security based upon wishful thinking rather than upon careful consideration, or he may have a sense of insecurity that is sometimes expressed as jealousy.

Test #6 – WORK

- An individual in love works for the other person or for their mutual benefit. He may study to make the other person proud of him. His ambition is spurred and he plans and saves for the future. He may daydream, but his dreams are reasonably attainable.

- An infatuated person may lose his ambition, his appetite, his interest in everyday affairs. He thinks of his own misery. He often daydreams, but his dreams are sometimes not limited to the attainable and are given free rein. At times the dreams become substitutes for reality and the individual lives in his world of dreams.

Test #7 – PROBLEM SOLVING

- A couple in love faces problems frankly and attempts to solve them. If there are barriers to their getting married, these barriers are approached intelligently and removed. Such as cannot be removed may be circumvented, but with the knowledge that what is done is deliberate circumvention.

- In infatuation, problems tend to be disregarded or glossed over.

Test #8 – DISTANCE

- Love tends to be constant.

- Infatuation often varies with the distance between the couple.

Talk It Over

1. Go way back into your memory and remember the first person you were infatuated with. Share that experience with your group and what it was that you were most infatuated with.

2. What is one way you show "phileo" love to your spouse or to a good friend?

    _____

    _____

    _____

3. Chip said that "agape" love is the reservoir out of which you can give "eros" or "phileo" love when you don't really feel like it. How do you nurture and develop "agape" love in a relationship?

    _____

    _____

    _____

4. What are some roadblocks or guardrails that married people need to put up so they don't get drawn into an infatuation with another person?

    _____

    _____

    _____

Live It Out – B.I.O.

BIO is a word that is synonymous with "life." Found in those three simple letters B.I.O. is the key to helping you become the person God wants you to be.

B = Come BEFORE GOD daily – To meet with Him personally through His word and prayer to enjoy His presence, receive His direction, and follow His will.

I = Do Life IN COMMUNITY weekly – Structuring your week to personally connect in safe relationships that provide love, support, transparency, challenge, and accountability.

O = Be ON MISSION 24/7 – Cultivating a mindset to "live out" Jesus' love for others through acts of sacrifice and service at home, work, play, and church.

COME BEFORE GOD

5. Read 1 Corinthians 13:4-8. Which quality of agape love most stands out to you? Why?

_____

_____

_____

DO LIFE IN COMMUNITY

6. If you had a friend come to you and confess that they were infatuated with someone at work, what would you say to them?

_____

_____

_____

BE ON MISSION

7. How can we help our kids and grandkids or nephews/nieces understand the difference between true love and infatuation?

_____

_____

_____

Accelerate (20 Minutes That Turn Concepts Into Convictions)

INSPIRATION comes from hearing God' Word; MOTIVATION grows by discussing God's Word; TRANSFORMATION occurs when you study it for yourself.

If you want to "accelerate" your growth, here is an assignment you can do this week. To help you get the most out of this exercise, consider partnering up with somebody in your group who will also commit to do the assignment this week. Then, after you have each done the assignment, agree to spend 10 minutes by phone to share what you learned and what you are applying.

COME BEFORE GOD

1. Carefully and slowly read the passage below from 1 Corinthians 13 (NIV).

    If I speak in the tongues of men or of angels, but do not have love, I am only a resounding gong or a clanging cymbal. If I have the gift of prophecy and can fathom all mysteries and all knowledge, and if I have a faith that can move mountains, but do not have love, I am nothing. If I give all I possess to the poor and give over my body to hardship that I may boast, but do not have love, I gain nothing.

    Love is patient, love is kind. It does not envy, it does not boast, it is not proud. It does not dishonor others, it is not self-seeking, it is not easily angered, it keeps no record of wrongs. Love does not delight in evil but rejoices with the truth. It always protects, always trusts, always hopes, always perseveres.

    Love never fails. But where there are prophecies, they will cease; where there are tongues, they will be stilled; where there is knowledge, it will pass away. For we know in part and we prophesy in part, but when completeness comes, what is in part disappears. When I was a child, I talked like a child, I thought like a child, I reasoned like a child. When I became a man, I put the ways of childhood behind me. For now we see only a reflection as in a mirror; then we shall see face to face. Now I know in part; then I shall know fully, even as I am fully known.

And now these three remain: faith, hope and love. But the greatest of these is love.

2.   Of all the things that Paul says love is "not," circle the ones that have a direct correlation to "pride."

3.   Verse 5 says that love does not dishonor others. Write out three ways that you can be unloving and dishonor others.

   •

   •

   •

4.   Verse 5 also says that love keeps no record of wrongs. Take a few moments to reflect on your relationships. Is there anyone that you are holding a grudge against? If so, what do you need to do in order to reconcile the relationship?

_____

_____

_____

5. Paul says in this passage that love protects. What does it look like practically to "have the back" of your friend or spouse?

_____

_____

_____

BE ON MISSION

6. Pick out a quality or two from this chapter and determine to live them out this coming week.

Session 4

HOW TO KNOW
IF YOU'RE IN LOVE

Part 2

HOW TO KNOW IF YOU'RE IN LOVE, PT. 2
Ephesians 5:1-2

Take It In (Watch the Video)

Test #9 – PHYSICAL ATTRACTION & INVOLVEMENT

- Physical attraction is a relatively smaller part of their total relationship when a couple is in love, a relatively greater part when they are infatuated. When a couple is in love, any physical contact they have tends to have meaning as well as be a pleasurable experience in and of itself. It tends to express what they feel toward each other.

- In infatuation, physical contact tends to be an end in itself. It represents only pleasurable experience devoid of meaning.

Test #10 – AFFECTION

- In love an expression of affection tends to come relatively late in the couple's relationship.

- In infatuation, it may come earlier, sometimes from the very beginning.

Test #11 – STABILITY

- Love tends to endure.

- Infatuation may change suddenly, unpredictably.

Test #12 – DELAYED GRATIFICATION

- A couple in love is not indifferent to the effects of postponement of their wedding and do not prolong the period of postponement unless they find it wiser to wait a reasonable time; they do not feel an almost irresistible drive toward haste.

- Infatuated couples tend to feel an urge toward getting married. Postponement is intolerable to them and they interpret it as deprivation rather than preparation.

Adapted from Marriage for
Moderns by Dr. Henry Bowman

HOW TO IMPROVE YOUR LOVE LIFE

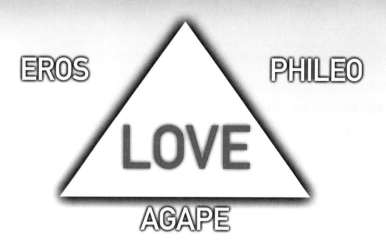

1. A word to singles – Keep your _____ and _____ involvement behind your leading from God and commitment to the other person.

2. A word to the married – Love requires the nourishment of all three kinds of love. Examine which one _____ _____ needs most and choose to give it as an act of worship to God.

Talk It Over

1. I want you to talk about what the Holy Spirit is saying to you from this session. And I want you to complete this statement… "I sense that God is asking me to…"

    _____

    _____

    _____

2. If a single friend asked you "how can I really know if the person I am dating is truly spiritual and committed to God." what would you say to them?

_____

_____

_____

3. Part of any healthy marriage is "phileo" love which is about companionship. What do you want and need when it comes to companionship with your spouse?

_____

_____

_____

4. What is one thing that can get in the way of you loving your spouse with "agape" love? What is one way that you can love your spouse with "agape" love?

_____

_____

_____

Live It Out – B.I.O.

BIO is a word that is synonymous with "life." Found in those three simple letters B.I.O. is the key to helping you become the person God wants you to be.

B = Come BEFORE GOD daily – To meet with Him personally through His word and prayer to enjoy His presence, receive His direction, and follow His will.

I = Do Life IN COMMUNITY weekly – Structuring your week to personally connect in safe relationships that provide love, support, transparency, challenge, and accountability.

O = Be ON MISSION 24/7 – Cultivating a mindset to "live out" Jesus' love for others through acts of sacrifice and service at home, work, play, and church.

COME BEFORE GOD

5. Chip said that in order to be a person that nurtures agape love in your marriage, you need to be a person that talks to God and is in His word. Honestly, how are you doing with that? And why is that important for marriage?

_____

_____

_____

DO LIFE IN COMMUNITY

6. Partner up with someone in your group and spend some time praying for each other's relationships.

BE ON MISSION

7. Identify one activity that will nurture "phileo" love and commit to put into practice this week.

- Take a leisurely walk

- Do a hobby together

- Talk about your dreams and goals for this year

- Share something that is a struggle or challenge

- Watch a movie together

- Take a drive

- Plan a weekend away together

- Go to the mall

- Watch a football game

- _____

Accelerate (20 Minutes That Turn Concepts Into Convictions)

INSPIRATION comes from hearing God' Word; MOTIVATION grows by discussing God's Word; TRANSFORMATION occurs when you study it for yourself.

If you want to "accelerate" your growth, here is an assignment you can do this week. To help you get the most out of this exercise, consider partnering up with somebody in your group who will also commit to do the assignment this week. Then, after you have each done the assignment, agree to spend 10 minutes by phone to share what you learned and what you are applying.

COME BEFORE GOD

1. Spend some time slowly reading this passage from 1 John 4:7-21 (NIV)

Dear friends, let us love one another, for love comes from God. Everyone who loves has been born of God and knows God. Whoever does not love does not know God, because God is love. This is how God showed his love among us: He sent his one and only Son into the world that we might live through him. This is love: not that we loved God, but that he loved us and sent his Son as an atoning sacrifice for our sins. Dear friends, since God so loved us, we also ought to love one another. No one has ever seen God; but if we love one another, God lives in us and his love is made complete in us.

This is how we know that we live in him and he in us: He has given us of his Spirit. And we have seen and testify that the Father has sent his Son to be the Savior of the world. If anyone acknowledges that Jesus is the Son of God, God lives in them and they in God. And so we know and rely on the love God has for us. God is love. Whoever lives in love lives in God, and God in them. This is how love is made complete among us so that we will have confidence on the day of judgment: In this world we are like Jesus. There is no fear in love. But perfect love drives out fear, because fear has to do with punishment. The one who fears is not made perfect in love.

We love because he first loved us. Whoever claims to love God yet hates a brother or sister is a liar. For whoever does not love their brother and sister, whom they have seen, cannot love God, whom they have not seen. And he has given us this command: Anyone who loves God must also love their brother and sister.

2.   What are some adjectives that you would use to describe God's love in this passage?

   •

   •

   •

   •

   •

3.   What does John mean when he says, "but if we love one another, God lives in us and His love is made complete in us" (v.12)?

   _____

   _____

   _____

4. How does "love drive out fear" (v.18)?

_____

_____

_____

DO LIFE IN COMMUNITY

5. If you are married, commit this week to extravagantly express love to your spouse. If you are single, commit to extravagantly express love to a friend.

BE ON MISSION

6. This week reach out to somebody who is not a Christian and show God's love by unexpectedly blessing them.

Session 5

LOVE AND SEX
WHY KNOWING THE DIFFERENCE MAKES ALL THE DIFFERENCE
Part 1

"LOVE AND SEX"
WHY KNOWING THE DIFFERENCE MAKES ALL THE DIFFERENCE

Take It In (Watch the Video)

Ephesians 5:3-6

* Lauren's Story

* Mike's Story

* Paula's Story

> When we fail to understand the difference between love and sex, we are doomed to failure in both our relationships and our sexuality.

* The Historical Setting - Paul's Day

* The Context - God's Concern for Our Relationships

Do not grieve the Holy Spirit of God, by whom you were sealed for the day of redemption.   Let all bitterness and wrath and anger and clamor and slander be put away from you, along with all malice.   Be kind to one another, tender-hearted, forgiving each other, just as God in Christ also has forgiven you.

Ephesians 4:30-32 (NASB)

Drs. Les & Leslie Parrot

- The Command = Walk in_____ . (vs. 1-4)

How?

1. Positively – Be giving, caring, sacrificial and _____ toward others.

   Therefore be imitators of God, as beloved children; and walk in love, just as Christ also loved you and gave Himself up for us, an offering and a sacrifice to God as a fragrant aroma.

   Ephesians 5:1-2 (NASB)

2. Negatively – Refuse to take, exploit, cheapen, defraud, or _____ sexual activity for genuine love and authentic intimacy.

Talk It Over

1. As you think about your childhood, how was sex viewed and talked about in your home?

   _____

   _____

   _____

2. How have the cultural messages about sex changed during your lifetime?

   _____

   _____

   _____

3. Chip said that all sin is not fundamentally about behavior, it is about relationship. How does that square with what you have been taught and what you have believed?

_____

_____

_____

4. If sin isn't fundamentally about behavior, but about relationship, what are the implications?

_____

_____

_____

Live It Out – B.I.O.

BIO is a word that is synonymous with "life." Found in those three simple letters B.I.O. is the key to helping you become the person God wants you to be.

B = Come BEFORE GOD daily – To meet with Him personally through His word and prayer to enjoy His presence, receive His direction, and follow His will.

I = Do Life IN COMMUNITY weekly – Structuring your week to personally connect in safe relationships that provide love, support, transparency, challenge, and accountability.

O = Be ON MISSION 24/7 – Cultivating a mindset to "live out" Jesus' love for others through acts of sacrifice and service at home, work, play, and church.

COME BEFORE GOD

5. Read Ephesians 4:17-19 which describes the kind of culture these Christians were living in. What word or phrases most stands out to you? What are the parallels between the culture in Ephesus and our culture today?

    _____

    _____

    _____

DO LIFE IN COMMUNITY

6. In Ephesians 4, Paul said that we are to be "tender-hearted" toward one another. In your small group, what does it look like practically to be tender-hearted toward one another?

    _____

    _____

    _____

BE ON MISSION

7. Chip said that as Christians we are "to be different but not weird." In our culture, what does it look like for us to be different but not weird?

    _____

    _____

    _____

Accelerate (20 Minutes That Turn Concepts Into Convictions)

INSPIRATION comes from hearing God's Word; MOTIVATION grows by discussing God' Word; TRANSFORMATION occurs when you study it for yourself.

If you want to "accelerate" your growth, here is an assignment you can do this week. To help you get the most out of this exercise, consider partnering up with somebody in your group who will also commit to do the assignment this week. Then, after you have each done the assignment, agree to spend 10 minutes by phone to share what you learned and what you are applying.

COME BEFORE GOD

1. Carefully read the following passage from Galatians 5:16-26 (NIV)

    So I say, walk by the Spirit, and you will not gratify the desires of the flesh. For the flesh desires what is contrary to the Spirit, and the Spirit what is contrary to the flesh. They are in conflict with each other, so that you are not to do whatever you want. But if you are led by the Spirit, you are not under the law.

    The acts of the flesh are obvious: sexual immorality, impurity and debauchery; idolatry and witchcraft; hatred, discord, jealousy, fits of rage, selfish ambition, dissensions, factions and envy; drunkenness, orgies, and the like. I warn you, as I did before, that those who live like this will not inherit the kingdom of God.

    But the fruit of the Spirit is love, joy, peace, forbearance, kindness, goodness, faithfulness, gentleness and self-control. Against such things there is no law. Those who belong to Christ Jesus have crucified the flesh with its passions and desires. Since we live by the Spirit, let us keep in step with the Spirit. Let us not become conceited, provoking and envying each other.

2. **According to this passage, what are some results of living in the Spirit?**

    _____

    _____

    _____

3. What does Paul mean when he says "if you are led by the Spirit, you are not under the law"?

_____

_____

_____

4. In verse 24, Paul says that those who belong to Christ "have crucified the flesh with its passions and desires." What does it mean that we have "crucified the flesh"?

_____

_____

_____

DO LIFE IN COMMUNITY

5. Have a conversation with a friend this week and discuss what it means to "walk in the spirit." As you get together, look up some other verses that talk about the role of the Holy Spirit in our lives.

BE ON MISSION

6. Select one of the fruits of the Spirit (v.22-23) and focus this week on living out that fruits of the Spirit.

Session 6

LOVE AND SEX
WHY KNOWING THE DIFFERENCE MAKES ALL THE DIFFERENCE
Part 2

"LOVE AND SEX", PT. 2
WHY KNOWING THE DIFFERENCE MAKES ALL THE DIFFERENCE

Take It In (Watch the Video)

1. Negatively – Refuse to take, exploit, cheapen, defraud, or substitute sexual activity for genuine love and authentic intimacy.

> But do not let **immorality**
>
>> or **any impurity**
>>
>> or **greed** even be named among you,
>>
>> as is proper among saints;
>
> and **no filthiness,**
>
>> **silly talk,**
>>
>> **coarse jesting**, which are not fitting,
>>
>> but rather **giving of thanks.**

2. The Reason = Sexual impurity _____ relationships.

> For this you know with certainty; that
>
>> no **immoral**
>>
>> or **impure person**
>>
>> or **covetous man,** (who is an idolater),
>>
>>> has an inheritance in the kingdom
>>>
>>> of Christ and God.
>
> Let no one **deceive** you
>
>> with **empty words,**
>>
>> for because of **these things** (mentioned above)
>>
>>> the **wrath of God comes** upon the sons of disobedience.

Ephesians 5:3-6 (NASB)

- Where Do You Go From Here?

  - A word to uninvolved singles

  - A word to involved singles

  - A word to those in crisis

  - A word to the married

  - A word of hope for all of us – Isaiah 1:18-19

Talk It Over

1. "How does viewing God as a good and loving Father change how you hear these warnings about sexual sin?"

   _____

   _____

   _____

2. Chip said that sexual purity isn't only about behavior, but it is also about thoughts and words. What are some practical steps people can take to guard against sexually impure thoughts?

   _____

   _____

   _____

3. Look again at Ephesians 5:3-4. After Paul commands us to refrain from immorality, impurity, sexual greed, filthiness, and coarse jesting, why does he tell us to "give thanks"? What does giving thanks have to do with sexual purity?

_____

_____

_____

4. When it comes to sex, what are some of the "empty words" (messages) in our culture that can "deceive" Christians?

_____

_____

_____

Live It Out – B.I.O.

BIO is a word that is synonymous with "life." Found in those three simple letters B.I.O. is the key to helping you become the person God wants you to be.

B = Come BEFORE GOD daily – To meet with Him personally through His word and prayer to enjoy His presence, receive His direction, and follow His will.

I = Do Life IN COMMUNITY weekly – Structuring your week to personally connect in safe relationships that provide love, support, transparency, challenge, and accountability.

O = Be ON MISSION 24/7 – Cultivating a mindset to "live out" Jesus' love for others through acts of sacrifice and service at home, work, play, and church.

COME BEFORE GOD

5. Read again Ephesians 5:5-6. Why do you think God speaks so strongly about sexual sin? And what does it mean practically that the "wrath of God comes upon the sons of disobedience"?

_____

_____

_____

DO LIFE IN COMMUNITY

6. In our pursuit of sexual purity, how can relationships with other believers be helpful?

_____

_____

_____

BE ON MISSION

7. As a group, brainstorm a list of the benefits of living a sexually pure life.

_____

_____

_____

Accelerate (20 Minutes That Turn Concepts Into Convictions)

INSPIRATION comes from hearing God' Word; MOTIVATION grows by discussing God's Word; TRANSFORMATION occurs when you study it for yourself.

If you want to "accelerate" your growth, here is an assignment you can do this week. To help you get the most out of this exercise, consider partnering up with somebody in your group who will also commit to do the assignment this week. Then, after you have each done the assignment, agree to spend 10 minutes by phone to share what you learned and what you are applying.

COME BEFORE GOD

1. Carefully read the following passage from 2 Samuel 11:1-5 (NIV)

    In the spring, at the time when kings go off to war, David sent Joab out with the king's men and the whole Israelite army. They destroyed the Ammonites and besieged Rabbah. But David remained in Jerusalem.

    One evening David got up from his bed and walked around on the roof of the palace. From the roof he saw a woman bathing. The woman was very beautiful, and David sent someone to find out about her. The man said, "She is Bathsheba, the daughter of Eliam and the wife of Uriah the Hittite." Then David sent messengers to get her. She came to him, and he slept with her. (Now she was purifying herself from her monthly uncleanness.)Then she went back home. The woman conceived and sent word to David, saying, "I am pregnant."

2. **Read 2 Samuel 11:6-27. What steps did David take to try and cover up his sexual sin?**

    _____

    _____

    _____

3. Read Proverbs 6:27-29. What do these verses teach about the certain consequences for sexual immorality?

    _____

    _____

    _____

4. Read 2 Samuel 12:1-23. What were some of the specific consequences David had to endure as a result of his sin with Bathsheba?

    _____

    _____

    _____

DO LIFE IN COMMUNITY

5. All of us need people who love us and love God enough to speak the truth to us. Read 2 Samuel 12:1-6. How did God use Nathan in David's life at this critical moment? If you had been Nathan, how would you have felt?

    _____

    _____

    _____

BE ON MISSION

6. Psalm 51 records David's heartfelt confession after he is confronted with his sin. What are you top three observations about David's confession in Psalm 51?

_____

_____

_____

Session 7

HOW TO BE
SEXUALLY PURE
IN A SEX-SATURATED
WORLD

Part 1

HOW TO BE SEXUALLY PURE IN A SEX-SATURATED SOCIETY
Ephesians 5:7-10

Take It In (Watch the Video)

Introduction – Five Facts About Sex!

1. Those who abstain from sexual intercourse before marriage report the highest levels of sexual satisfaction in marriage.

2. Those who cohabitate (live together) before marriage have a 50% higher divorce rate than those who do not.

3. Those who abstain from sexual intercourse before marriage have the highest rates of fidelity in marriage.

4. The introduction of sex in a dating relationship almost always ushers in the "break-up" of that relationship.

5. Sexually transmitted diseases (including AIDS) can remain dormant for up to a decade or more; but be passed on to others during that time.

- Loving Relationships Demand Sexual Purity

  Walk in Love

  and walk in love, just as Christ also loved you, and gave Himself up for us, an offering and a sacrifice to God as a fragrant aroma. But do not let immorality or any impurity or greed not even be named among you, as is proper among saints; and there must be no filthiness and silly talk, or coarse jesting, which are not fitting, but rather giving of thanks.

  Ephesians 5:2-4 (NASB)

  For this you know with certainty, that no immoral or impure person or covetous man, who is an idolater, has an inheritance in the kingdom of Christ and God. Let no one deceive you with empty words, for because of these things the wrath of God comes upon the sons of disobedience.

  Ephesians 5:5-6 (NASB)

1.Bathesda Research Group, Washington Post

2. UCLA study

3. University South Carolina study

4. Dr.s Les & Leslie Parrott

Walk in the Light

Therefore do not be partakers with them; for you were formerly darkness, but now you are light in the Lord; walk as children of light (for the fruit of the light consists in all goodness and righteousness and truth), trying to learn what is pleasing to the Lord.

Ephesians 5:7-10 (NASB)

Talk It Over

1. How is your time in God's word? And what can you do to make this a higher priority in your life?

   _____

   _____

   _____

2. Romans 12:2 (NIV) says, "Do not conform to the pattern of this world, but be transformed by the renewing of your mind. Then you will be able to test and approve what God's will is—His good, pleasing and perfect will." What does this verse have to do with sexual purity? And, how do we "renew" our minds?

   _____

   _____

   _____

3. Chip said the word "partakers" has in it the idea that we are not to even associate with those things that pull us toward sexual impurity. Living in the 21st century, what does it look like practically to not "associate" with things that are sexually impure?

_____

_____

_____

4. At the beginning of this session Chip said "the more I love God the less appetite I will have for sexual impurity." What are one or two ways that help you deepen your love for God?

_____

_____

_____

Live It Out – B.I.O.

BIO is a word that is synonymous with "life." Found in those three simple letters B.I.O. is the key to helping you become the person God wants you to be.

B = Come BEFORE GOD daily – To meet with Him personally through His word and prayer to enjoy His presence, receive His direction, and follow His will.

I = Do Life IN COMMUNITY weekly – Structuring your week to personally connect in safe relationships that provide love, support, transparency, challenge, and accountability.

O = Be ON MISSION 24/7 – Cultivating a mindset to "live out" Jesus' love for others through acts of sacrifice and service at home, work, play, and church.

COME BEFORE GOD

5. Read Romans 13:11-14. As you think about sexual purity, what most stands out to you from this passage?

_____

_____

_____

DO LIFE IN COMMUNITY

6. Sexual purity is not just about managing external temptations. It is also about my internal heart and desires and character. How could your group help you in your journey to love God and "be" the right kind of person?

_____

_____

_____

BE ON MISSION

7. What can you do to help your kids and grandkids guard against sexual impurity?

_____

_____

_____

Accelerate (20 Minutes That Turn Concepts Into Convictions)

INSPIRATION comes from hearing God' Word; MOTIVATION grows by discussing God's Word; TRANSFORMATION occurs when you study it for yourself.

If you want to "accelerate" your growth, here is an assignment you can do this week. To help you get the most out of this exercise, consider partnering up with somebody in your group who will also commit to do the assignment this week. Then, after you have each done the assignment, agree to spend 10 minutes by phone to share what you learned and what you are applying.

COME BEFORE GOD

1. Carefully read the following passage from 1 Thessalonians 4:1-8 (NIV)

   As for other matters, brothers and sisters, we instructed you how to live in order to please God, as in fact you are living. Now we ask you and urge you in the Lord Jesus to do this more and more. For you know what instructions we gave you by the authority of the Lord Jesus.

   It is God's will that you should be sanctified: that you should avoid sexual immorality; that each of you should learn to control your own body in a way that is holy and honorable, not in passionate lust like the pagans, who do not know God; and that in this matter no one should wrong or take advantage of a brother or sister. The Lord will punish all those who commit such sins, as we told you and warned you before. For God did not call us to be impure, but to live a holy life. Therefore, anyone who rejects this instruction does not reject a human being but God, the very God who gives you his Holy Spirit.

2. Paul said it is God's will that we should be sanctified. What does it mean to be "sanctified"? Read this verse in some other translations.

_____

_____

_____

3. Circle all of the words in this passage that are your responsibility when it comes to sexual purity.

_____

_____

_____

4. Read Colossians 3:1-11. How does Colossians 3:1-4 help us in our pursuit of sexual purity?

_____

_____

_____

DO LIFE IN COMMUNITY

5. Paul challenged us to "avoid" sexual immorality. Have a conversation with a friend this week about ways you can "avoid" the temptation of sexual impurity.

_____

_____

_____

BE ON MISSION

6. Take a few moments and write out your prayer of commitment to sexual purity.

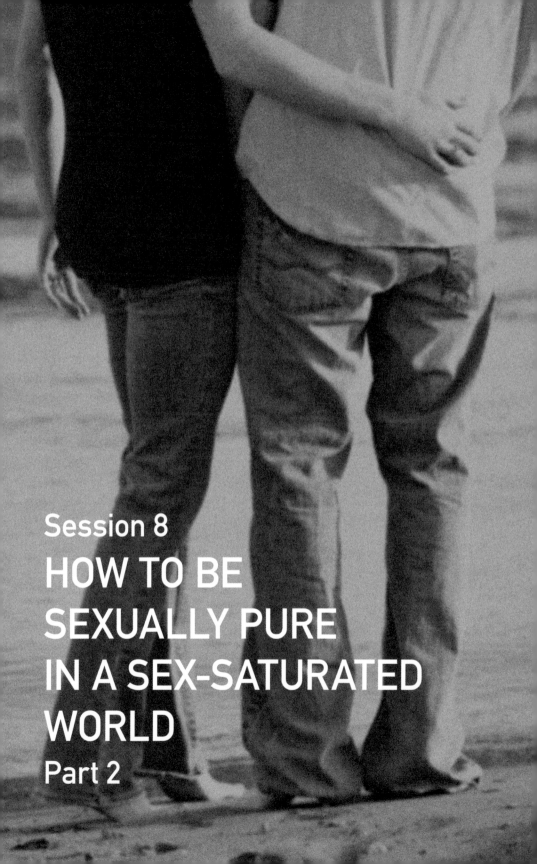

Session 8

HOW TO BE SEXUALLY PURE IN A SEX-SATURATED WORLD
Part 2

HOW TO BE SEXUALLY PURE IN A SEX-SATURATED SOCIETY, PT. 2
Ephesians 5:7-10

Take It In (Watch the Video)

- Sexual Purity Demands a Game Plan

    1. Develop _____ !
        Purity requires a personal commitment to the truth. (vs. 2-4)

    2. Ponder the _____ .
        Fear can be a legitimate and healthy motivator for delayed gratification.
        (vs. 5-6)

    3. Make _____ .
        Advanced decision making is an absolute necessity for sexual purity.
        (vs. 7-9)

    4. Get _____ .
        Asking others to help you keep your commitments to God will empower
        you to walk "pleasing to the Lord." (vs. 10)

- The Reward – Sexual Purity's Pay-off

    1. One couple's journey – God's way _____ !

    2. You can start today – It's never_____ !

    3. A word to virgins – You are not_____ ; you are wise!

Talk It Over

1. Of the four step game plan Chip shared, which one most resonates with you
    personally? And why?

    _____

    _____

    _____

2. The first step in creating a game plan for sexual purity is to develop convictions. When it comes to sexual purity what is a biblical conviction that you hold?

_____

_____

_____

If you have a mixed group with both men and women, split up for the rest of the discussion time. This will allow people to have more candid discussion with those of the same sex.

3. If you were to have a moral failure, what are the potential consequences that are most sobering and potentially devastating to you?

_____

_____

_____

4. Chip said we underestimate the fear of God. For you, how much does the fear of God play into your pursuit of sexual purity?

_____

_____

_____

Live It Out – B.I.O.

BIO is a word that is synonymous with "life." Found in those three simple letters B.I.O. is the key to helping you become the person God wants you to be.

B = Come BEFORE GOD daily – To meet with Him personally through His word and prayer to enjoy His presence, receive His direction, and follow His will.

I = Do Life IN COMMUNITY weekly – Structuring your week to personally connect in safe relationships that provide love, support, transparency, challenge, and accountability.

O = Be ON MISSION 24/7 – Cultivating a mindset to "live out" Jesus' love for others through acts of sacrifice and service at home, work, play, and church.

COME BEFORE GOD

5. In 1 Corinthians 6:18 (NIV) Paul says, "Flee from sexual immorality. All other sins a person commits are outside the body, but whoever sins sexually, sins against their own body." In your everyday life, how do you practically "flee from sexual immorality"?

    _____

    _____

    _____

DO LIFE IN COMMUNITY

6. Chip shared several pre-decisions he has made. Which one of Chip's pre-decisions is perhaps one you should adopt? And, are there other pre-decisions that you should have for your life?

    _____

    _____

    _____

BE ON MISSION

7. Chip said accountability is inviting someone else to help you keep your commitments. What would it look like for you to have accountability in your pursuit of sexual purity?

_____

_____

_____

8. Do you sense that God is calling you to make some kind of change or commitment? If so, share it with your group and close this session by praying for one another.

_____

_____

_____

Accelerate (20 Minutes That Turn Concepts Into Convictions)

INSPIRATION comes from hearing God' Word; MOTIVATION grows by discussing God's Word; TRANSFORMATION occurs when you study it for yourself.

If you want to "accelerate" your growth, here is an assignment you can do this week. To help you get the most out of this exercise, consider partnering up with somebody in your group who will also commit to do the assignment this week. Then, after you have each done the assignment, agree to spend 10 minutes by phone to share what you learned and what you are applying.

COME BEFORE GOD

1. **Carefully read the following passage from Proverbs 5 (NIV).**

    My son, pay attention to my wisdom,
      turn your ear to my words of insight,
    that you may maintain discretion
      and your lips may preserve knowledge.
    For the lips of the adulterous woman drip honey,
      and her speech is smoother than oil;
    but in the end she is bitter as gall,
      sharp as a double-edged sword.
    Her feet go down to death;
      her steps lead straight to the grave.
    She gives no thought to the way of life;
      her paths wander aimlessly, but she does not know it.
    Now then, my sons, listen to me;
      do not turn aside from what I say.
    Keep to a path far from her,
      do not go near the door of her house,
    lest you lose your honor to others
      and your dignity to one who is cruel,
    lest strangers feast on your wealth
      and your toil enrich the house of another.
    At the end of your life you will groan,
      when your flesh and body are spent.
    You will say, "How I hated discipline!
      How my heart spurned correction!
    I would not obey my teachers
      or turn my ear to my instructors.
    And I was soon in serious trouble
      in the assembly of God's people."
    Drink water from your own cistern,
      running water from your own well.
    Should your springs overflow in the streets,
      your streams of water in the public squares?
    Let them be yours alone,
      never to be shared with strangers.
    May your fountain be blessed,

and may you rejoice in the wife of your youth.
A loving doe, a graceful deer—
   may her breasts satisfy you always,
   may you ever be intoxicated with her love.
Why, my son, be intoxicated with another man's wife?
   Why embrace the bosom of a wayward woman?
For your ways are in full view of the Lord,
   and he examines all your paths.
The evil deeds of the wicked ensnare them;
   the cords of their sins hold them fast.
For lack of discipline they will die,
   led astray by their own great folly.

2.   Many consequences are listed in this chapter for engaging in sexual immorality. What are the three consequences that are most sobering for you, personally?

-

-

-

3.   What are some of the strategies Solomon shares that can keep us from being seduced into immorality?

-

-

-

4.   As you reflect on this passage, is there any sexual sin that you need to repent of? If so, spend some time in prayer and confession.

_____

_____

_____

DO LIFE IN COMMUNITY

5. This week Chip talked about making pre-decisions that will keep you from sexual impurity. Develop your own list of pre-decisions and share them with a close friend.

BE ON MISSION

6. Chip also challenged us to ponder the consequences of sexual immorality. Take some time to reflect on this and then write out what the consequences would be if you had a moral failure.

Session 9

WAKE UP WORLD! THERE'S A BETTER WAY TO DO RELATIONSHIPS

Part 1

WAKE UP WORLD! THERE'S A BETTER WAY TO DO RELATIONSHIPS

Take It In (Watch the Video)

Ephesians 5:11-14

> Where there is no revelation,
> the people cast off restraint;
> but blessed is he who keeps the law.
>
> Proverbs 29:18 (NIV)

A Night I Will Always Remember

- A private war was raging

- A small farmhouse in the country

- A young couple beginning God's journey together

- An ordinary moment with extraordinary impact

- A "vision" that changed my life

WHY IS SEX SUCH SERIOUS BUSINESS TO GOD?
Ephesians 5:11-14 (NASB)

The Command

And do not participate in the unfruitful deeds of darkness, but instead even expose them;

verse 11

The Reason =

...for it is disgraceful even to speak of the things which are done by them in secret.

verse 12

The Explanation

But all things become visible when they are exposed by the light, for everything that becomes visible is light.

verse 13

The Invitation

For this reason it says,
"Awake, sleeper,
And arise from the dead,
And Christ will shine on you."

verse 14

Summary

Just as light silently reveals all things for what they really are; so it is when God's people MODEL purity and love in relationships – they expose SEXUAL immorality for what it really is…lustful, destructive, self-worship.

Talk It Over

1. Think about Chip's illustration of the flashlight and us "being" the light. How could you and your group "be" the light when it comes to sexual purity and modeling loving relationships?

_____

_____

_____

2. If you were the pastor of your church, how would you help your congregation pursue sexual purity?

_____

_____

_____

3. Chip's experience with Dave and Lanny gave him a vision for what a loving and pure family looked like. Who has been that kind of example in your life?

_____

_____

_____

4. How might you influence a young person or young couple to have a vision for a godly family life?

_____

_____

_____

Live It Out – B.I.O.

BIO is a word that is synonymous with "life." Found in those three simple letters B.I.O. is the key to helping you become the person God wants you to be.

B = Come BEFORE GOD daily – To meet with Him personally through His word and prayer to enjoy His presence, receive His direction, and follow His will.

I = Do Life IN COMMUNITY weekly – Structuring your week to personally connect in safe relationships that provide love, support, transparency, challenge, and accountability.

O = Be ON MISSION 24/7 – Cultivating a mindset to "live out" Jesus' love for others through acts of sacrifice and service at home, work, play, and church.

COME BEFORE GOD

5. In Ephesians 5:11-13 Paul commands us to not participate in sexual immorality and he challenges us to be the light. Why do you think he follows that command with the words, Awake, sleeper, And arise from the dead, And Christ will shine on you.

    _____

    _____

    _____

DO LIFE IN COMMUNITY

6. In Ephesians 5:11 Paul said that we are to expose the unfruitful deeds of darkness. How do we accomplish that in a loving, winsome, grace-filled way?

    _____

    _____

    _____

BE ON MISSION

7. Spend some time as a group praying for your families, your churches, your school systems, and your community.

    _____

    _____

    _____

Accelerate (20 Minutes That Turn Concepts Into Convictions)

INSPIRATION comes from hearing God' Word; MOTIVATION grows by discussing God's Word; TRANSFORMATION occurs when you study it for yourself.

If you want to "accelerate" your growth, here is an assignment you can do this week. To help you get the most out of this exercise, consider partnering up with somebody in your group who will also commit to do the assignment this week. Then, after you have each done the assignment, agree to spend 10 minutes by phone to share what you learned and what you are applying.

COME BEFORE GOD

1. Carefully read Romans 13:11-14 (NIV)

   And do this, understanding the present time: The hour has already come for you to wake up from your slumber, because our salvation is nearer now than when we first believed. The night is nearly over; the day is almost here. So let us put aside the deeds of darkness and put on the armor of light. Let us behave decently, as in the daytime, not in carousing and drunkenness, not in sexual immorality and debauchery, not in dissension and jealousy. Rather, clothe yourselves with the Lord Jesus Christ, and do not think about how to gratify the desires of the flesh.

To understand the context of these verses, go back and read Romans 13:1-10.

2. What does Paul mean when he says our "salvation is nearer now than when we first believed"?

   _____

   _____

   _____

3. What do you think Paul is referring to when he challenges us to "put on the armor of light"?

    _____

    _____

    _____

4. What does it mean practically to clothe yourself with Jesus Christ?

    _____

    _____

    _____

DO LIFE IN COMMUNITY

5. Have a conversation this week with a good friend about two issues.

    •   What does it look like every day to clothe yourself with Jesus Christ?

    •   How are you tempted when it comes to gratifying the desires of the flesh.

    Pray for one another and commit to check in and hold each other accountable.

BE ON MISSION

6. Titus talks about making the teaching about God "attractive." Make it your commitment this week, by the way you live, to make the gospel attractive to those around you.

Session 10

WAKE UP WORLD! THERE'S A BETTER WAY TO DO RELATIONSHIPS

Part 2

WAKE UP WORLD! THERE'S A BETTER WAY TO DO RELATIONSHIPS, PT. 2

Take It In (Watch the Video)

Ephesians 5:11-14

Answering God's Call to "The Second Sexual Revolution"

1. A revolutionary way to _____ about human sexuality

   • Sex is _____ . Hebrews 13:4 (NASB)

   • Sex is _____ . 1 Corinthians 6:15-20 (NASB)

2. A revolutionary way to _____ the opposite sex.

   • God's way – 1 Peter 3:3-4 (NASB)

      • I – _____ _____

      • O – _____ _____

      • U – _____ _____

3. A revolutionary way to _____ to the opposite sex.

   • As a _____ . John 15:13 (NASB)

   • As a _____ _____ . 1 Timothy 5:1-2 (NASB)

   • As a _____ _____ _____ . Hebrews 10:24 (NASB)

Questions to consider

1. Why is sex such serious business in God's eyes? What is at stake for the world around us?

    _____

    _____

    _____

2. In what ways do you need to change how you think about sex? What implications does this have on your thought life? Behavior? Viewing habits? Renewing of your mind?

    _____

    _____

    _____

3. How does modesty facilitate loving and lasting relationships? In what ways has "our culture" seduced us into attracting the opposite sex in ways that prohibit focus on inner vs. outward qualities?

    _____

    _____

    _____

Talk It Over

1. Chip said we have to think differently about sex. And he said sex is sacred. How is sex "sacred"?

    _____

    _____

    _____

2. Read 1 Corinthians 6:15–20. What is most striking to you from this passage?

    _____

    _____

    _____

3. What does it mean that your body is the temple of the Holy Spirit? And what are the practical implications of that truth?

    _____

    _____

    _____

4. In Job 31:1 Job says that he made a covenant with his eyes. When it comes to sexual purity, what does it mean to make a covenant with your eyes? And what are the implications for your viewing habits?

    _____

    _____

    _____

Live It Out – B.I.O.

BIO is a word that is synonymous with "life." Found in those three simple letters B.I.O. is the key to helping you become the person God wants you to be.

B = Come BEFORE GOD daily – To meet with Him personally through His word and prayer to enjoy His presence, receive His direction, and follow His will.

I = Do Life IN COMMUNITY weekly – Structuring your week to personally connect in safe relationships that provide love, support, transparency, challenge, and accountability.

O = Be ON MISSION 24/7 – Cultivating a mindset to "live out" Jesus' love for others through acts of sacrifice and service at home, work, play, and church.

COME BEFORE GOD

5. Read 1 Peter 3:3-4 where Peter is helping Christian women know how to reach their unbelieving husbands. So when it comes to starting a Second Sexual Revolution that Chip talked about, how can we do it in a way that is winsome and attractive?

_____

_____

_____

DO LIFE IN COMMUNITY

6. What is your personal single biggest takeaway from this series?

_____

_____

_____

7. How could you answer God's call to The Second Sexual Revolution? What might that look like in your life and relationships?

_____

_____

_____

SMALL GROUP
LEADER RESOURCES

Group Agreement

People come to groups with a variety of different expectations. The purpose of a group agreement is simply to make sure everyone is on the same page and that we have some common expectations.

The following Group Agreement is a tool to help you discuss specific guidelines during your first meeting. Modify anything that does not work for your group. Then be sure to discuss the questions in the section called Our Game Plan. This will help you to have an even better group experience!

We Agree To The Following Priorities:

Take the Bible Seriously	To seek to understand and apply God's truth in the Bible
Group Attendance	To give priority to the group meeting (call if I am going to be absent or late)
Safe Environment	To create a safe place where people can be heard and feel loved (no snap judgments or simple fixes)
Respectful Discussion	To speak in a respectful and honoring way to our mate and others in the group
Be Confidential	To keep anything that is shared strictly confidential and within the group
Spiritual Health	To give group members permission to help me live a godly, healthy spiritual life that is pleasing to God
Building Relationships	To get to know the other members of the group and pray for them regularly
Pursue B.I.O.	To encourage and challenge each other in "coming before God", "doing life together in community" and "being on mission 24/7"
Prayer	To regularly pray with and for each other
Other	_____

Our game plan:

1. What day and time will we meet? _____

2. Where will we meet? _____

3. How long will we meet each week? _____

4. What will we do for refreshments? _____

5. What will we do about childcare? _____

Tips for Facilitating Your Group Meeting

Before the group arrives

1. BE PREPARED. Your personal preparation can make a huge difference in the quality of the group experience. We strongly suggest previewing both the DVD teaching by Chip Ingram and the study guide.

2. PRAY FOR YOUR GROUP MEMBERS BY NAME. Ask God to use your time together to touch the heart of every person in your group. Expect God to challenge and change people as a result of this study.

3. PROVIDE REFRESHMENTS. There's nothing like food to help a group relax and connect with each other. For the first week, we suggest you prepare a snack, but after that, ask other group members to bring the food so that they share in the responsibilities of the group and make a commitment to return.

4. RELAX. Don't try to imitate someone else's style of leading a group. Lead the group in a way that fits your style and temperament. Remember that people may feel nervous showing up for a small group study, so put them at ease when they arrive. Make sure to have all the details covered prior to your group meeting, so that once people start arriving, you can focus on them.

Take It In (Watch the Video)

1. GET THE VIDEO READY. Each video session will be between 15 and 20 minutes in length. Go ahead and cue up the video so that you can just push "play" when you are ready to watch the session.

2. **HAVE AMPLE MATERIALS.** Before you start the video, also make sure everyone has their own copy of the study guide. Encourage the group to open to this week's session and follow along with the teaching. There is an outline in the study guide with an opportunity to fill in the outline.

3. **ARRANGE THE ROOM.** Set up the chairs in the room so that everyone can see the television. And, arrange the room in such a way that it is conducive to discussion.

Talk It Over

Here are some guidelines for leading the discussion time:

1. **MAKE THIS A DISCUSSION,** not a lecture. Resist the temptation to do all the talking, and to answer your own questions. Don't be afraid of a few moments of silence while people formulate their answers.

   And don't feel like you need to have all the answers. There is nothing wrong with simply saying "I don't know the answer to that, but I'll see if I can find an answer this week."

2. **ENCOURAGE EVERYONE TO PARTICIPATE.** Don't let one person dominate, but also don't pressure quieter members to speak during the first couple of sessions. Be patient. Ask good follow up questions and be sensitive to delicate issues.

3. **AFFIRM PEOPLE'S PARTICIPATION AND INPUT.** If an answer is clearly wrong, ask "What led you to that conclusion?" or ask what the rest of the group thinks. If a disagreement arises, don't be too quick to shut it down! The discussion can draw out important perspectives, and if you can't resolve it there, suggest researching it further and return to the issue next week.

   However, if someone goes on the offensive and engages in personal attack, you will need to step in as the leader. In the midst of spirited discussion, we must also remember that people are fragile and there is no place for disrespect.

4. **DETOUR WHEN NECESSARY.** If an important question is raised that is not in the study guide, take time to discuss it. Also, if someone shares something personal and emotional, take time for them. Stop and pray for them right then. Allow the Holy Spirit room to maneuver, and follow His prompting when the discussion changes direction.

5. **SUBGROUP.** One of the principles of small group life is "when numbers go

up, sharing goes down." So, if you have a large group, sometimes you may want to split up into groups of 4-6 for the discussion time. This is a great way to give everyone, even the quieter members, a chance to share. Choose someone in the group to guide each of the smaller groups through the discussion. This involves others in the leadership of the group, and provides an opportunity for training new leaders.

6.   PRAYER. Be sensitive to the fact that some people in your group may be uncomfortable praying out loud. As a general rule, don't call on people to pray unless you have asked them ahead of time or have heard them pray in public. But this can also be a time to help people build their confidence to pray in a group. Consider having prayer times that ask people to just say a word or sentence of thanks to God.

Live It Out — B.I.O.

At this point in each week's session, you will engage the B.I.O. pathway. B.I.O. is a process that is designed to help Christians live like Christians. As you integrate these three vital practices into your life, it will result in spiritual momentum and help you thrive as a follower of Jesus.

- Come "BEFORE GOD" Daily - To meet with Him personally through His Word and prayer, in order to enjoy His Presence, receive His direction, and follow His will.

- Do Life "IN COMMUNITY" Weekly - Structuring your week to personally connect in safe relationships that provide love, support, transparency, challenge, and accountability.

- Be "ON MISSION" 24/7 - Cultivating a mindset to "live out" Jesus' love for others through acts of sacrifice and service at home, work, play and church.

Accelerate (20 Minutes That Turn Concepts Into Convictions)

INSPIRATION comes from hearing God's Word; MOTIVATION grows by discussing God's Word; TRANSFORMATION occurs when you study it for yourself.

This 20 minute exercise is meant to be done apart from the group meeting. It is a great way to go deeper with the material and turbo charge people's growth. You can lead the way by personally doing the Accelerate section each week. And then encourage others to join and take a few moments in your group meeting to talk about what people have been learning from this section.

Love, Sex and Lasting Relationships Session Notes

Welcome to this series called Love, Sex, and Lasting Relationships. We all know that we live in a sex-saturated society. And we are also painfully aware that sexual impurity and broken relationships are rampant in our generation. Through this series, you are going to help lead your group to discover God's plan and path for meaningful sex, true love, and great relationships.

Whether you are brand new at leading a small group or you are a seasoned veteran, God is going to use you. God has a long history of using ordinary people to get His work done.

These brief notes are intended to help prepare you for each week's session. By spending just a few minutes each week previewing the video and going over these session notes you will set the table for a great group experience. Also, don't forget to pray for your group each week.

SESSION 1 – THE SECRET TO A LASTING RELATIONSHIP, PT. 1

- If your group doesn't know each other well, be sure that you spend some time getting acquainted. Don't rush right into the video lesson. Remember, small groups are not just about a study or a meeting, they are about relationships.

- If this is a new group, be sure to capture everyone's contact information. It is a good idea to send out an e-mail with everybody's contact information so that the group can stay in touch. At the back of your study guide is a roster where people can fill in the names and contact information of the other group members.

- When you are ready to start the session, be sure that each person in your group has a copy of the study guide. The small group study guide is important for people to follow along and to take notes.

- Spend a little time in this first session talking about B.I.O. These three core practices are the pathway to maturity. You will see these letters and terms throughout this curriculum. Start getting your group comfortable with the concepts of "coming before God", "doing life together in community", and "being on mission".

- Facilitating the discussion time. Sometimes Chip will ask you as the facilitator to lead the way by answering the first question. This allows you to lead by example and your willingness to share openly about your life will help others feel the permission to do the same.

- Before you wrap up your group time in this first session, be sure to introduce the Accelerate exercise in the study guide. This is an assignment they can do during the week that will help turbo charge their growth. Encourage them to find a partner in the group who they can talk to each week about the accelerate exercise.

- The first question your group will discuss this week will be to identify the most dominant messages from Hollywood about love, sex, and relationships. Don't let this time turn into a rant about our culture. The point is to identify the kind of messages Hollywood is promoting when it comes to sex and relationships.

- The fourth question this week will explore how our identity in Christ impacts our view of love and sex. You might want to look up a few verses about our identity in Christ to be able to share with the group.

SESSION 2 – THE SECRET TO A LASTING RELATIONSHIP, PT. 2

- Why not begin your preparation by praying right now for the people in your group. You might even want to keep their names in your Bible. You may also want to ask people in your group how you can pray for them specifically.

- If somebody doesn't come back this week, be sure and follow up with them. Even if you knew they were going to have to miss the group meeting, give them a call or shoot them an e-mail letting them know that they were missed. It would also be appropriate to have a couple of other people in the group let them know they were missed.

- If you haven't already previewed the video, take the time to do so. It will help you know to best facilitate the group and what are the best discussion questions for your group.

- Ask good follow up questions… the only thing better than a good question is a good follow up question. Think of your group discussion like an onion. Each good follow up question allows you to pull back another layer to get them and get down beneath the surface.

- This week Chip is going to challenge your group with a little assignment. If people are married or they are single and in a relationship, he will ask them grab some time this week over lunch or a cup of coffee and talk about the five layers in the pyramid diagram. Encourage your group to take this assignment seriously and then be sure to follow up next week to see how it went.

- The Do Life in Community question this week asks "how can this group help you be a more whole and healthy person?" Being in a small group isn't just about doing a study together. It is about loving and helping each other live out the Christian life. This is a great question to help your group explore how they can support one another.

SESSION 3 – HOW TO KNOW IF YOU'RE IN LOVE, PT. 1

- Did anybody miss last week's session? If so, make it a priority to follow up and let them know they were missed. It just might be your care for them that keeps them connected to the group.

- Don't be afraid of silence. We don't like dead time, do we? It makes us feel uncomfortable. To be a good facilitator, you must learn to get comfortable with silence. Silence gives people a moment to process and figure out what they want to say. If you move on too quickly, you miss some of the best input.

- Think about last week's meeting for a moment. Was there anyone that didn't talk or participate? In every group there are extroverts and there are introverts. There are people who like to talk and then there are those who are quite content NOT to talk. Not everyone engages in the same way or at the same level but you do want to try and create an environment where everyone wants to participate.

- Follow up with your group this week to see how they did with the Accelerate assignment this week. Don't shame or embarrass anyone who didn't get to the assignment, but honestly challenge them to make this a priority in the coming week.

- In this session Chip will talk a lot about the difference between love and infatuation. It can seem like this session is mostly focused on single people. So, if you have a group of married couples, focus on Chip's definition of love and help them to assess how they are doing at living those out in their marriage.

- Be sure that you spend some time on question four this week. Your group will be asked to identify some roadblocks or guardrails that married people need to put up so they don't get drawn into an infatuation with another person.

SESSION 4 – HOW TO KNOW IF YOU'RE IN LOVE, PT. 2

- Don't feel any pressure to get through all the questions. As people open up and talk, don't move on too quickly. Give them the space to consider what is going on inside them as they interact with this teaching.

- Share the load. One of the ways to raise the sense of ownership within the group is to get them involved in more than coming to the meeting. So, get someone to help with refreshments… find somebody else to be in charge of the prayer requests… get someone else to be in charge of any social gathering you plan… let someone else lead the discussion one night. Give away as much of the responsibility as possible. That is GOOD leadership.

- If your group is not sharing as much as you would like or if the discussion is being dominated by a person or two, try subgrouping. If your group is 8 people or more, this is a great way to up the level of participation. After watching the video teaching, divide the group into a couple of smaller groups for the discussion time. It is good to get someone you think would be a good facilitator to agree to this ahead of time.

- This week you are going to start the discussion time a little differently. The opening question will ask people to respond to what they have heard in the teaching. Chip will ask them to complete the statement "I sense that God is asking me to…" It might be helpful if you have watched the video ahead of time and are prepared to share first.

- At the close of this session Chip will talk about the fact that some of us can't experience true love in our relationships because we are harboring unforgiveness and resentment. Encourage people to really deal with this if there is unforgiveness in their relationship. This could be the breakthrough that some couples need in order to truly experience agape love.

SESSION 5 – LOVE AND SEX: WHY KNOWING THE DIFFERENCE MAKES ALL THE DIFFERENCE, PT. 1

- You are now at the halfway point of this series. How is it going? How well is the group connecting? What has been going well and what needs a little work? Are there any adjustments you need to make?

- Confidentiality is crucial to group life. The moment trust is breached, people will shut down and close up. So, you may want to mention the importance of confidentiality again this week just to keep it on people's radar.

- Each time your group meets take a few minutes to update on what has happened since the last group meeting. Ask people what they are learning and putting into practice. Remember, being a disciple of Jesus means becoming a "doer of the word".

- Revisit the importance of B.I.O. this week. Reinforce the importance of people integrating these core practices in their lives. For example, talk about the priority of coming before God each day and submitting to the authority of God's truth.

- Don't chase rabbits. This happens in every group. You will ask a discussion and someone will take you down a trail that really isn't relevant to the discussion. It is your job as the group leader to discern when you need to bring the group back. Here is how I often handle that situation… I will look for a moment to jump in and say "Hey, this is great discussion but I want to come back to our topic and focus our discussion there."

- In this session Chip will talk about God's view of sex and how the world has distorted and perverted God's gift. As Christians we can be lured into sexual sin. Chip will state that "all sin is fundamentally not about rules, but about relationship". Make sure to spend some time talking about this truth. Understanding and embracing this truth can have huge implications for our ability to resist temptation.

SESSION 6 – LOVE AND SEX: WHY KNOWING THE DIFFERENCE MAKES ALL THE DIFFERENCE, PT. 2

- One way to deepen the level of community within your group is to spend time together outside the group meeting. If you have not already done so, plan something that will allow you to get to know each other better. Also, consider having someone else in the group take responsibility for your fellowship event.

- As you begin this week's session, do a check-in to see what people are learning and applying from this series. Don't be afraid to take some time at the beginning of your meeting to review some key ideas from the previous week's lessons.

- Consider asking someone in your group to facilitate next week's lesson. Who knows, there might be a great potential small group leader in your group. It will give you a break and give them a chance to grow.

- Your job is not to lead a good meeting. Your job is to help develop those in your group into mature followers of Jesus. So, encourage people to take a next step in their growth. Don't just ask them what they could do, ask them what they WILL do. We don't grow by talking about obedience, we grow by "obeying" and being "doers of the word."

- This session has a more sober and serious feel to it. Help the people in your group feel the seriousness of sexual sin while also helping them know there is hope and help in Christ.

- In the Do Life in Community question this week, your group will be asked "how can relationships with other believers be helpful?" The truth is, we all need help and accountability to remain sexually pure. Talk through practical ways you can help each other.

SESSION 7 – HOW TO BE SEXUALLY PURE IN A SEX-SATURATED SOCIETY, PT. 1

- Consider sending an e-mail to each person in your group this week letting them know you prayed for them today. Also, let them know that you are grateful that they are in the group.

- Take a few minutes this week before you get into the study to talk about the impact of this series so far. Ask people what they are learning, applying, and changing in their lives. For this series to have lasting impact it has to be more than just absorbing information. So, challenge your group to put what they are learning into action.

- It is often a good idea to take a week break and do something different. This also helps the group understand that small group is more than just a meeting. You might consider taking one night off from your group meeting to just have dinner together and share/celebrate how God has used this series in your lives. Or, you could take a night off from your group meeting to do your ministry project and "do good" for someone in need.

- One of the most powerful tools we have for remaining sexually pure is the word of God. As we allow God's truth to saturate our minds and thinking, God will begin to change our character and our desires. We don't change our lustful thoughts by just trying hard. We change our lustful thoughts by renewing our minds with God's truth. So, really challenge your group to take this seriously and ask them to commit to daily time in God's word.

SESSION 8 – HOW TO BE SEXUALLY PURE IN A SEX-SATURATED SOCIETY, PT. 2

- As you begin this week's discussion time, be sure to follow up on the challenge last week to spend time in God's word. Ask people how it went and how God spoke to them this past week.

- This session is going to be very straightforward and practical. Chip will talk about the need to have a game plan for remaining sexually pure. Make sure you have plenty of time in your discussion to talk through these practical strategies.

- Chip will also talk about the need for accountability in order to stay sexually pure. Sometimes the word accountability has some baggage attached to it and people can feel like it is an interrogation. Reinforce the definition Chip gave you that accountability is me inviting someone else to help me keep my commitments. It is important that every one of us have somebody in our life that can speak the hard truth to us and ask us the hard questions.

- Chip will also talk about the value in Christian counseling. For some, there is still a stigma attached to counseling. Help your group see the value and benefit of seeking some help for your marriage.

- After the first two discussion questions, you will be asked to split up the group by men and women for the rest of the discussion time. This will allow people to have a more candid discussion with those of the same sex.

SESSION 9 – WAKE UP WORLD! THERE'S A BETTER WAY TO DO RELATIONSHIPS, PT. 1

- Since this is the next to the last week of this study, you might want to spend some time this week talking about what your group is going to do after your complete this study. You might even consider having a computer available where your group can go to livingontheedge.org and explore other small group studies from Chip.

- In this session Chip will talk about starting a second sexual revolution. This is a hope-filled message about what "could be" if we would do sex and love God's way. When we look at the world around us, sometimes we can feel hopeless and discouraged. And while your group may not change the entire culture of Hollywood, they can have great influence in their own homes and spheres of influence.

- The final part of the discussion this week is dedicated to prayer. Your group will be asked to spend some time praying for your families, churches, school systems and community. Make sure to leave adequate time to pray.

SESSION 10 – WAKE UP WORLD! THERE'S A BETTER WAY TO DO RELATIONSHIPS, PT. 2

- "Thanks" for you willingness to lead this group… and thanks for your faithfulness in investing in those in your group. And I hope you have grown and been blessed by this material and by the people in your group.

- Be sure that you everyone is clear what your group is doing next after this study.

- In this final session, question 4 talk about a verse in Job, where Job said he made a covenant with his eyes. The group will be asked to discuss what it means to make a covenant with your eyes and what the implications are for their viewing habits. This is a huge issue. So, help people think through healthy guidelines and decisions for what they watch. It would also be good to talk about guidelines we need to have in place for our kids.

- Question 6 this week asks people to identify their personal biggest takeaway from this series. Be sure to leave some time for this question and to celebrate how God has used this series in the lives of your group members.

Prayer and Praise

One of the most important things you can do in your group is to pray with and for each other. Write down each other's concerns here so you can remember to pray for these requests during the week!

Use the Follow Up box to record an answer to a prayer or to write down how you might want to follow up with the person making the request. This could be a phone call, an e-mail or a card. Your personal concern will mean a lot!

Date	Person	Prayer Request	Follow Up

Date	Person	Prayer Request	Follow Up

LOVE, SEX AND LASTING RELATIONSHIPS

Date	Person	Prayer Request	Follow Up

Date	Person	Prayer Request	Follow Up

LOVE, SEX AND LASTING RELATIONSHIPS

Group Roster

Name	Home Phone	Email

What's Next?
More Group Studies from Chip Ingram:

Balancing Life's Demands
Biblical Priorities for a Busy Life

Busy, tired and stressed out? Learn how to put "first things first" and find peace in the midst of pressure and adversity.

BIO
How to Become An Authentic Disciple of Jesus

Unlock the Biblical DNA for spiritual momentum by examining the questions at the heart of true spirituality.

Culture Shock
A Biblical Response to Today's Most Divisive Issues

Bring light—not heat—to divisive issues, such as abortion, homosexuality, sex, politics, the environment, politics and more.

Doing Good
What Happens When Christians Really Live Like Christians

This series clarifies what Doing Good will do in you and then through you, for the benefit of others and the glory of God.

Effective Parenting in a Defective World
Raising Kids that Stand Out from the Crowd

Packed with examples and advice for raising kids, this series presents Biblical principles for parenting that still work today.

Experiencing God's Dream for Your Marriage
Practical Tools for a Thriving Marriage

Examine God's design for marriage and the real life tools and practices that will transform it for a lifetime.

Five Lies that Ruin Relationships
Building Truth-Based Relationships

Uncover five powerful lies that wreck relationships and experience the freedom of understanding how to recognize God's truth.

Watch previews and order at livingontheedge.org or 888.333.6003.

The Genius of Generosity
Lessons from a Secret Pact Between Friends
The smartest financial move you can make is to invest in God's Kingdom. Learn His design for wise giving and generous living.

God As He Longs for You to See Him
Seeing God With 20/20 Vision
A deeper look at seven attributes of God's character that will change the way you think, pray and live.

Good to Great in God's Eyes
10 Practices Great Christians Have in Common
If you long for spiritual breakthrough, take a closer look at ten powerful practices that will rekindle a fresh infusion of faith.

Heaven
It's Not What You Think
Chip Ingram digs into scripture to reveal what heaven will be like, what we'll do there, and how we're to prepare for eternity today.

Holy Ambition
Turning God-Shaped Dreams Into Reality
Do you long to turn a God-inspired dream into reality? Learn how God uses everyday believers to accomplish extraordinary things.

House or Home: Marriage Edition
God's Blueprint for a Great Marriage
Get back to the blueprint and examine God's plan for marriages that last for a lifetime.

House or Home: Parenting Edition
God's Blueprint for Biblical Parenting
Timeless truths about God's blueprint for parenting, and the potential to forever change the trajectory of your family.

Watch previews and order at livingontheedge.org **or** 888.333.6003.